A MAZE
OF GRACE

claiming God's grace during a season of suffering

PAUL CHAPPELL

First published in 2005 by Striving Together Publications, a
ministry of Lancaster Baptist Church, Lancaster, CA 93535.
Striving Together Publications is committed to providing
tried, trusted, and proven books that will further equip
local churches to carry out the Great Commission. Your
comments and suggestions are valued.

Striving Together Publications
4020 E. Lancaster Blvd.
Lancaster, CA 93535
800.201.7748

Edited by Cary Schmidt
Cover design by Jeremy Lofgren
Layout by Craig Parker

ISBN 978-0-9726506-4-9

Printed in the United States of America

Table of Contents

When God wants to drill a man,
And thrill a man,
And skill a man;
When God wants to mold a man
To play the noblest part,

When He yearns with all His heart
To create so great and bold a man
That all the world shall be amazed,
Watch His methods, watch His ways
How He ruthlessly perfects
Whom He royally elects.

How He hammers him and hurts him,
And with mighty blows, converts him
Into trial shapes of clay
Which only God understands,
While his tortured heart is crying,
And he lifts beseeching hands.

How He bends but never breaks
When his good He undertakes.
How He uses whom He chooses,
And with every purpose fuses him,
By every act, induces him
To try His splendor out.
God knows what he's about.

—Anonymous

CHAPTER ONE

Finding My Way

The fixed heart is the secret of courage.
—G. Campbell Morgan

Amazing grace, how sweet the sound, and how easy to sing either at the moment of our salvation from a wretched past, in time of great blessing, or in expectation of the exceeding joy we shall still be experiencing even when we've been there for 10,000 years. But what about the "every days" which fill our lives? What about when real struggle and loss threaten our sanity, our homes, and our faith—times when "Amazing Grace" seems more like a "maze of grace" marked by tears and questioning?

Many people have memorized the familiar words and strengthening music of John Newton's classic hymn, "Amazing Grace," at least the first and fourth stanzas so often sung in churches wherever Christ's name is preached. However, few know the words of the stanzas in between, or that this precious hymn of the faith actually has twelve stanzas. The first stanza heralds the grace of salvation and rises to a praiseworthy declaration of our heavenly hope in the final stanza. But what of the stanzas in between? Did John Newton really pen the words "through many dangers, toils, and snares" and "when this flesh and heart shall fail"? Certainly he did, and yet the suffering which he acknowledged in a Christian's life is followed by startling statements such as "'Tis grace hath brought me safe thus far, and grace will lead me home," and "He will my shield and portion be, as long as life endures." Our recognition of God's grace leading us, even in our seasons of suffering, helps us to endure even when our faith wanes.

The first stirrings of faith, whether experiences as a child or as an adult, often focus upon the grace of God which forgives us of our sins, and the love of God, which forgets them.

> *For by grace are ye saved through faith; and that not of yourselves: it is the gift of God: Not of works, lest any man should boast.*—Ephesians 2:8-9

The perfect love of Christ, manifested through His abundant grace on our behalf, leads us to salvation. However, it is a small number indeed who understand the continuing work of grace, which transforms the life of a believer. God's grace not only saves us, but it also keeps us. It strengthens and enables us to serve Him and to live a life more abundant for *"God is able to make all grace abound toward [us],"* the Bible affirms in 2 Corinthians 9:8.

"In every need," God says, "I want to do an inner working in you. I want to create a disposition in you called grace. So that as you face this trial, you can tap into an inner, spiritual resource that you would not have had, had you never received me as your personal Saviour." As we grow in grace, we grow in daily consciousness of this fact: God is our sufficiency. He has gone

before, and He supplies all grace, and His grace
abounds. God's grace is available to help us
remain humble when we are feeling strong.
God's grace is available to build us up when we
feel hurt or weak. When we are limited, God's
grace is unlimited, and often His grace visits us
in circumstances that seem absent of the very
grace that will carry us through our difficulty
or challenge. When the circumstances are most
confusing, we must cling to grace, for there
is nothing a counselor, psychologist or even a
good, well-intentioned friend can do for us in
comparison to what God can accomplish in our
hearts by His grace. This response is a courageous
one, and courage is an affair of the heart. Only a
heart fixed upon God is able to glean the healing,
restorative power of the Scriptures. Only the
courageous soul will *"not be afraid of evil tidings:
[for] his heart is fixed, trusting in the LORD,"* and
the promises of His Word (Psalm 112:7). Second
Corinthians 4:7–9 and 15 testify,

> *But we have this treasure in earthen
> vessels, that the excellency of the power
> may be of God, and not of us. We are*

troubled on every side, yet not distressed;
we are perplexed, but not in despair;
Persecuted, but not forsaken; cast down,
but not destroyed; For all things are
for your sakes, that the abundant grace
might through the thanksgiving of many
redound to the glory of God.

As Christians, we are possessors of a great treasure—the presence of the Lord Jesus Christ in us, in the earthen vessel which is our body. We are fragile. Our bodies are but a vapor in time. They become weary, weak, or sick, and at an appointed time, they die. When our earthen vessels are broken, opportunity is given for the gift of His presence and the grace of His love to flow out from us—covering our weaknesses, conquering our fears, and touching others as evidence of His love and mercy in a lost and dying world. Our brokenness can be overwhelming, but we have this promise: God will never try us above what we are able.

There hath no temptation taken you but
such as is common to man: but God is
faithful, who will not suffer you to be

*tempted above that ye are able; but will
with the temptation also make a way to
escape, that ye may be able to bear it.*
—1 Corinthians 10:13

We must trust in God, just as children trust in a loving parent. An attentive parent will know how much his child can carry physically, and so our Heavenly Father knows how much we can carry physically, emotionally, mentally, and spiritually. His grace is dependable. Without acknowledging God's strength and sufficiency in our lives, we are crushed by our burdens, victims of our circumstances, and subjects to bitterness.

The Bible records the story of a man named Paul who may have been the greatest Christian to ever inhabit this planet, but he had weaknesses and many trials. One in particular led him to call upon God…

*For though I would desire to glory, I shall
not be a fool; for I will say the truth: but
now I forbear, lest any man should think
of me above that which he seeth me to
be, or that he heareth of me. And lest I
should be exalted above measure through*

*the abundance of the revelations, there was given to me a thorn in the flesh, the messenger of Satan to buffet me, lest I should be exalted above measure. For this thing I besought the Lord thrice, that it might depart from me. And he said unto me, **My grace is sufficient for thee:** for my strength is made perfect in weakness. Most gladly therefore will I rather glory in my infirmities, that the power of Christ may rest upon me. Therefore I take pleasure in infirmities, in reproaches, in necessities, in persecutions, in distresses for Christ's sake: for when I am weak, then am I strong.*—2 Corinthians 12:6-10

Paul served the Lord fervently and was used greatly to accomplish God's purposes in his generation. Of all people, Paul could have reacted to his "thorn in the flesh" and questioned, doubted, or accused God. Instead, he responded to God, and in his infirmity, necessity, and distress he recognized God's grace and sufficiency. **He gained balance instead of bitterness.** There is some speculation as to what exactly Paul's "thorn in the flesh" was. Whatever it was, it was real to him, just as our infirmities, necessities, and distresses are real to us. We believe in a God who remains the same yesterday, today, and forever. Because of this we know that God's response to Paul is His healing response to us today. God will not always isolate us from harm, but He will always surround us with His grace, which is sufficient in ALL THINGS. God is the adequate resource; the Way for us to make it through our present trials. He didn't say He would give us the way, show us the way, or point us in the right direction. He said, **"I am your way** in this life and in eternity."

> *Jesus saith unto him, I am the way, the*
> *truth, and the life: no man cometh unto*
> *the Father, but by me.*—John 14:6

Paul had a real affliction. He asked not once, but three times that God would remove it. He questioned within himself why his ministry and life should be limited by such an infirmity.

*Men seek an explanation of suffering in
cause and effect. They look backward
for a connection between prior sin
and present suffering. The Bible looks
forward in hope and seeks explanations,
not so much in origins as in goals. The
purpose of suffering is seen, not in its
cause, but in its results"*—Francis I.
Anderson, *Job*.

God did not give Paul an explanation;
He gave him promises. He gives us the same
promises…

*And he said unto me, My grace is
sufficient for thee: for my strength is made
perfect in weakness. Most gladly therefore
will I rather glory in my infirmities, that
the power of Christ may rest upon me.*
—2 Corinthians 12:9

*Blessed be God, even the Father of
our Lord Jesus Christ, the Father of
mercies, and the God of all comfort; Who
comforteth us in all our tribulation, that
we may be able to comfort them which are*

*in any trouble, by the comfort wherewith
we ourselves are comforted of God. For
as the sufferings of Christ abound in us,
so our consolation also aboundeth by
Christ.*—2 Corinthians 1:3-5

As we allow ourselves to be comforted by the grace of God, we can become a comfort to others and a testimony of God's sufficiency. Let us allow God's grace to flood our souls and to overflow our lives as a witness to others. His blessing is upon us, *"For this God is our God for ever and ever: he will be our guide even unto death"*—Psalm 48:14.

*I can read my affliction as a correction,
or as a mercy, and I confess I know not
how to read it. How should I understand
this illness? I cannot conclude, though
death conclude me. If it is a correction
indeed, let me translate it and read it as
a mercy; for though it may appear to be
a correction, I can have no greater proof
of your mercy than to die in thee and by
that death to be united to him who died
for me.*—John Donne, *Devotions*

CHAPTER TWO

Caterpillars Don't Fly

And straightway the father of the child
cried out, and said with tears, Lord, I
believe; help thou mine unbelief.
—Mark 9:24

Can we benefit from adversity? Does the butterfly
need to struggle free of its cocoon to develop the
muscle in its wings required for sweet flight? The
answer is yes. Most of us don't seek adversity, but
all of us do experience it in some measure. When
adversity comes we all face a choice. Will we be
enslaved to our adversity and become embittered

by our circumstances? Will we allow our adversity to serve us by leading us to depend more fully on God, taking opportunity to evaluate our motives and priorities?

> *Sometimes I went so far as to thank destiny for the privilege of such loneliness, for only in solitude could I have scrutinized my past so carefully, or examined so closely my interior and outward life. What strong and strange new germs of hope were born in my soul during those memorable hours! I weighed and decided all sorts of issues, I entered into a compact with myself to avoid the errors of former years and the rocks on which I had been wrecked.*
> —Fyodor Dostoyevski, *The House of the Dead*

Adversity is a call to self-examination, for both the one who suffers and those who witness the adverse circumstance. Self-examination creates in us a desire to know God intimately, to pray spontaneously, and to witness willingly. Suffering also fosters a renewed and appropriate sense of humility, and motivates us to adopt an eternal perspective. Our adversities can become stepping-stones to increased faith, rather than stumbling blocks of disappointment and despair.

> *Humble yourselves therefore under the mighty hand of God, that he may exalt you in due time: Casting all your care upon him; for he careth for you. Be sober, be vigilant; because your adversary the devil, as a roaring lion, walketh about, seeking whom he may devour: Whom resist stedfast in the faith, knowing that the same afflictions are accomplished in your brethren that are in the world. But the God of all grace, who hath called us unto his eternal glory by Christ Jesus, after that ye have suffered a while, make you perfect, stablish, strengthen, settle you.*—1 Peter 5:6–10

These verses from 1 Peter 5 equip Christians to face the dangers of loss and adversity that threaten our faith. So often we take for granted our health, families, and friends. We treat our tomorrows as promises instead of gifts. When adversity strikes, first we must take into account who we are and Who God is, and trust the only promises we do have—the promises of His Word which assure us that if we humble ourselves "under [His] mighty hand," He will exalt us in due time. He will lift us up (James 4:10).

Second, we must acknowledge our vulnerability. Adversity is no respecter of persons, and neither is the Devil, who takes pleasure in "kicking people when they're down." The ultimate goal of our adversary, the Devil, is to destroy and to devour us.

> *Be sober, be vigilant; because your*
> *adversary the devil, as a roaring lion,*
> *walketh about, seeking whom he may*
> *devour:*—1 Peter 5:8

Physical, mental, and emotional trials are only tools that he cunningly wields in an effort to undercut our faith. As a Christian, the Devil knows he has lost us for eternity, but, if he can tempt us to deny or doubt God when we are injured, he can use us to scar the testimony of the Lord Jesus Christ. When adversity causes us to lose our balance, we can fall to our knees in prayer. Recognize our real adversary, and steadfastly resist him in the faith. We are not alone. Jesus is God with us, and He is in us. We are not singled out for affliction. Other Christians too are experiencing suffering, and this suffering gives way to glory.

Our suffering is not senseless. Our suffering will lead to glory if we allow the God of all grace to complete in us the work He began at salvation. This work is conformity to the image of His dear Son, Christ Jesus. This perfect work purposes to establish, strengthen, and settle us. By grace we gain maturity, and our maturing is preparation for that upward call into His eternal glory.

> *And I said, Oh that I had wings like a dove! for then would I fly away, and be at rest.*—Psalm 55:6

God is always at work in our lives, even in our pain. So often we read about heroes of the faith and marvel at the big assignments they received from God and accomplished for His glory. We see the pain, the struggle, and even the loss they endured, and wonder. We must keep in mind that while the Bible is full of accounts of the big assignments God entrusted to His servants, volumes could be filled with the unpublished details of little assignments. Assignments that prepared them for a task God had ordained. The ministries for which these servants of God volunteered required them to submit to the special challenges that accompany Christian service.

For example, Amy Carmichael is a twentieth century hero of the faith. Although it took her almost a decade (full of little assignments) to "find herself" on the mission field, she quickly made up for lost time and attacked the large assignments with fervor and faith as an advocate for temple children in Hindu India. Her extensive work was centered in sound evangelism and social ministry; however, she was challenged greatly both by pressures from the Hindu nationals, dissension among workers, criticism from outsiders, and finally physical trauma. A serious fall causing internal injuries and a badly broken foot placed Amy in her bed where she remained confined until her death. While in her bed, **by faith**, Amy produced a small library of autobiographical literature that has inspired and chastened each succeeding generation of Christians. *"By it, [she] being dead, yet speaketh…"* (Hebrews 11:4c).

> *Accept, for yourself, the Fatherhood of God, which is only possible for you and me because of the sacrifice of the blessed Son, our Saviour. **And by the presence of the Holy Spirit within, you will learn to rejoice in the Word of God, and nothing else.** This, then, is the call to the soul that would ascend above all earthly circumstance, to walk in heavenly places: leave yourself open to the circumstances of His choice, for that is perfect acceptance. Rest in the Word of God.*—Amy Carmichael, *You Are My Holy Place*

We cannot foresee what God has ordained for our today or tomorrow, but we can let the adversity we experience have its perfecting work in our lives. Let us pray to be established, rather than beg for the escape. Caterpillars don't fly until they have endured the struggle. Our "wings" are formed and strengthened in the struggles too!

Don't excuse yourself from the blessings, which are hidden for only a season. The God of all grace does not allow suffering to destroy our faith, but to develop our wings. So struggle, then fly, and through it all, be at rest. God, help us pray as David did…

> *It is good for me that I have been*
> *afflicted; that I might learn thy statutes.*
> *Before I was afflicted I went astray: but*
> *now have I kept thy word. Thou art good,*
> *and doest good; teach me thy statutes.*
> —Psalm 119:71, 67–68

CHAPTER THREE

Wildflowers and Stars

You do not have to sit outside in the dark.
If, however, you want to look at the stars,
you will find that darkness is required.
—Annie Dillard

The simple perfection of a wildflower and the
secret wonder of a star evoke different responses
from different people, and yet they do not
change. Some pick flowers; others admire them
from a distance. Some wish upon a star, while
others study them through a lens, but both
the wildflower and the star are common parts

of our experience. Suffering too is a common part of our experience, but as Christians our responses should be anything but common. Many people use their adversities as excuses to distance themselves from God, but the purpose of adversity is to draw us closer to Him.

> *Beloved, think it not strange concerning the fiery trial which is to try you, as though some strange thing happened unto you: But rejoice, inasmuch as ye are partakers of Christ's sufferings; that, when his glory shall be revealed, ye may be glad also with exceeding joy. If ye be reproached for the name of Christ, happy are ye; for the spirit of glory and of God resteth upon you: on their part he is evil spoken of, but on your part he is glorified. Yet if any man suffer as a Christian, let him not be ashamed; but let him glorify God on this behalf. Wherefore let them that suffer according to the will of God commit the keeping of their souls to him in well doing, as unto a faithful Creator.*—1 Peter 4:12–14, 16, 19

The Bible promises that each of us will experience seasons of suffering. This suffering can come in many forms such as personal struggles, sickness, death of loved ones, financial pressures, broken trusts, physical pain, and strained relationships. All of these circumstances bring heaviness to our spirit and a need for healing. This scripture from 1 Peter 4 administers a spiritual prescription for suffering. From it we may learn what our responses to adversity should be.

The Bible asserts that suffering and times of sorrow are not strange to the Christian experience. Our Lord wore a crown of thorns, and yet many Christians somehow think that the promise of eternal life and a guarantee for carefree living accompany one another. The Scriptures make no such claim. In fact, Jesus testified of the opposite when He said,

> *These things I have spoken unto you, that* **in me ye might have peace.** *In the world* **ye shall have tribulation:** *but be of good cheer; I have overcome the world.*
> —John 16:33

The Christian's peace is not from the absence of suffering, but from the constant abiding presence of the Lord within throughout the struggle. God does not single people out for persecution. He promises the comfort of His presence by His Holy Spirit in the pain.

Nobody wants to "make a joyful noise" when they are suffering, and they don't want anybody else to tell them to either. Yet, the Bible does instruct the Christian to *"rejoice evermore, pray without ceasing,* [and] *in every thing give thanks: for this is the will of God in Christ Jesus concerning* [us]" (1 Thessalonians 5:16–18).

In response to suffering and the Bible's admonition to rejoice, we must first consider the love of God. We must reflect upon His love, which motivated Him to suffer on a cross to purchase our salvation—a love that now sustains us through the gift of His Holy Spirit. God loves us and will never express Himself in any other way but love toward us. Each of us must determine in his own heart to view his circumstances always against the backdrop of the Cross. We love Him because He first loved us, even in adversity. Joy is a grace-induced response to suffering. It may not occur on the first day or during the first month, but the sooner it comes, the sooner our spiritual healing begins.

It is a common myth that all suffering in a Christian's life has a traceable lineage to a hidden sin. This may or may not be the case. Certainly adverse circumstances should prompt us toward self-examination and confession of known sin. But after this, we should acknowledge that the Bible teaches that suffering is not always a form of chastisement. Sometimes it is an indication that the faith of the suffering one is mature enough to bear the difficulty for God's glory. God gives a special gift of grace, an anointing to those who suffer, to aid and to comfort. We need not be ashamed when we suffer, especially when the struggle depletes our emotional, spiritual, physical, and mental strength. Paul also experienced this struggle-related fatigue, yet he testified, *"all things are for* [our] *sakes that the abundant grace might through the thanksgiving of many redound to the glory of God. For which cause **we faint not; but though our outward man perish, yet the inward man is renewed day by day"***—2 Corinthians 4:15–16.

This daily renewal through the indwelling Spirit of God is a promise. So claim the promise, experience the renewal, take each day one minute at a time, and draw on the sustaining power of God, who raised Christ Jesus from the dead.

A prayerful gospel chorus, which is often used in worship, requests…

> *Lord, prepare me to be a sanctuary*
> *Pure and holy*
> *Tried and true*
> *With thanksgiving, I'll be a living*
> *Sanctuary for You.*

It is easy to sing the words, "Lord, prepare me to be a sanctuary." It takes commitment to continue and sing "pure and holy," but it is extremely difficult to ask for the "tried and true." It is a miracle of grace when we can do so "with thanksgiving," truly becoming a living sanctuary—a living sacrifice—for Him and for His glory.

> *I beseech you therefore, brethren, by the*
> *mercies of God, that ye present your*
> *bodies a living sacrifice, holy, acceptable*

*unto God, which is your reasonable
service. And be not conformed to this
world: but be ye transformed by the
renewing of your mind, that ye may
prove what is that good, and acceptable,
and perfect, will of God. For I say,
through the grace given unto me, to every
man that is among you, not to think of
himself more highly than he ought to
think; but to think soberly, according
as God hath dealt to every man the
measure of faith.*—Romans 12:1–3

This response to suffering is only possible when we know God well enough to trust Him as our faithful and loving Creator.

God didn't just fling the stars into space; He made sure they wouldn't run into each other. The Bible says that He is upholding all things by the power of His hand. If the sun were even a few miles closer or farther away from the earth, we would either burn up or freeze. The Scriptures reveal that He numbers the hairs on our heads. He watches over the sparrow, and clothes the field with grass. Have you ever wondered who planted the wild flowers? God is both a faithful and loving Creator. Just as His hand upholds all created things, His heart upholds our spirits always, even unto the end of the world…

In times of trouble I say,

1. *He brought me here. It is by His will that I am in this difficult place, and in that will I rest.*
2. *He will keep me here in His love, and give me grace in this trial to behave as His child.*
3. *He will make this trial a blessing, and teach me lessons He intended for me to learn by working in me the grace He means to bestow.*
4. *In His good time, He will bring me out again. How and when He knows, and in His knowing I trust.*

—Andrew Murray

CHAPTER FOUR

If You Had Been There

*You ascended from before our eyes, and
we turned back grieving, only to find you
in our hearts.*—Augustine

To us, the Bible seems full of paradoxes, but that
is only because our eternal viewpoint is so limited.
One needs to look no further than the Beatitudes
to wonder at the wisdom of God.

*Blessed are they that mourn: for they
shall be comforted.*—Matthew 5:4

The simplicity of the statement begs the question, "Wouldn't I be better comforted if I didn't have to mourn at all?" However, it is in our times of mourning and sorrow that God reveals Himself to us, **through us**.

God is about the business of conforming us to the image of Jesus, Who is "God with us." As Christians (Christ-like ones), our suffering is a tool by which we learn obedience and faith. It is also an opportunity to experience God's love in a way not yet known and to increase in the knowledge of His sufficiency and provision. The older we become and the longer we live, the more vulnerable we are to sorrow and difficulty. Some choose to react and isolate themselves from possible hurt, but in doing so they escape the joys of life only found in service and relationship with others. Whenever we enter the presence of joy, we become candidates for sorrow. God never denied sorrow as a part of our lives, but He does transform our sorrow into victory. That is why He says, *"Blessed are they that mourn."* God does not promise the absence of adversity, or prompt us to live as hermits to avoid sorrow. Rather, He encourages us with the assurance of His presence as we abide in Him.

The Bible reveals three distinct types of mourning. Natural mourning, in the event of death or injury of a loved one, is a necessary part of the healing process. Unnatural mourning or false guilt, however, distracts us from life as we focus on what is either untrue or irreconcilable about a past relationship or event. Such mourning can hinder our recovery and isolate us from accepting the love of those who would seek to minister to and comfort us. Spiritual mourning or godly sorrow is the common experience of all Christians at one time or another. It often begins as conviction and prompts repentance—a change in our minds concerning our spiritual condition that produces a change in our actions.

> *The LORD is nigh unto them that are of a broken heart; and saveth such as be of a contrite spirit. Many are the afflictions of the righteous: but the LORD delivereth him out of them all.*—Psalm 34:18–19

Two particular women in the Scriptures experienced great mourning. Their story offers a lesson and encouragement to us all.

*Now a certain man was sick, named Lazarus, of Bethany, the town of **Mary and her sister Martha.** (It was that Mary which anointed the Lord with ointment, and wiped his feet with her hair, whose brother Lazarus was sick.) Therefore his sisters sent unto him, saying, Lord, behold, he whom thou lovest is sick. When Jesus heard that, he said, This sickness is not unto death, but for the glory of God, that the Son of God might be glorified thereby. Now Jesus loved Martha, and her sister, and Lazarus. When he had heard therefore that he was sick, he abode two days still in the same place where he was. Then after that saith he to his disciples, Let us go into Judaea again. These things said he: and after that he saith unto them, Our friend Lazarus sleepeth; but I go, that I may awake him out of sleep.*

*Then said his disciples, Lord, if he sleep, he shall do well. Howbeit Jesus spake of his death: but they thought that he had spoken of taking of rest in sleep. Then said Jesus unto them plainly, Lazarus is dead. And I am glad for your sakes that I was not there, to the intent ye may believe; nevertheless let us go unto him. Then when Jesus came, he found that he had lain in the grave four days already. Now Bethany was nigh unto Jerusalem, about fifteen furlongs off: And many of the Jews came to Martha and Mary, to comfort them concerning their brother. Then Martha, as soon as she heard that Jesus was coming, went and met him: but Mary sat still in the house. Then said Martha unto Jesus, **Lord, if thou hadst been here, my brother had not died.***
—John 11:1-7, 11-15, 17-21

Martha's sister, Mary, had a similar response…

Now Jesus was not yet come into the town, but was in that place where

> *Martha met him. The Jews then*
> *which were with her in the house, and*
> *comforted her, when they saw Mary,*
> *that she rose up hastily and went out,*
> *followed her, saying, She goeth unto the*
> *grave to weep there. Then when Mary*
> *was come where Jesus was, and saw him,*
> *she fell down at his feet, saying unto*
> *him,* **Lord, if thou hadst been here, my**
> **brother had not died.**—John 11:30-32

Martha and Mary were believers, and yet in the midst of their great sorrow and loss, they questioned the Lord. In their grief they accused Him. They were followers of Jesus. They had watched Him heal the lame, give sight to the blind, and forgive sin. And yet at a crucial moment they each wavered, and it was at that point that the Lord addressed them. Jesus did not defend Himself. He had no need. Instead, Jesus came to the heart of the matter when He spoke to Martha…

> *Jesus said unto her, I am the resurrection,*
> *and the life: he that believeth in me,*
> *though he were dead, yet shall he live:*

*And whosoever liveth and believeth in
me shall never die. **Believest thou this?**
She saith unto him, Yea, Lord: I believe
that thou art the Christ, the Son of God,
which should come into the world.*
—John 11:25–27

Jesus addressed Martha concerning her
faith, not her trial. He asked, "Do you believe?"
Martha's eyes probably closed as she surveyed her
heart and sighed saying, "Yes, Lord. I do believe
in You." **It was in response to her faith that Jesus
was able to accomplish what He had set out
to do, which was to raise Lazarus.** Then Jesus
asked…

*And said, Where have ye laid him? They
said unto him, Lord, come and see. Jesus
wept. **Then said the Jews, Behold how
he loved him! And some of them said,
Could not this man, which opened
the eyes of the blind, have caused that
even this man should not have died?**
Jesus therefore again groaning in himself
cometh to the grave. It was a cave, and
a stone lay upon it. Jesus said, Take ye*

*away the stone. Martha, the sister of him
that was dead, saith unto him, Lord, by
this time he stinketh: for he hath been
dead four days. Jesus saith unto her, Said
I not unto thee, that, if thou wouldest
believe, thou shouldest see the glory of
God?*—John 11:34-40

Even though Martha did not know what God
was doing, His purpose had been firm when Jesus
set out for Judea, and yet it remained intact. **The
only variable in the situation was the faith of
Mary and Martha.** Jesus was saying to them, "I
love you. My love for you is not and will never
be, a question. You know that I can heal the sick
and make the lame walk; however, you do not yet
know that I can raise the dead. This experience,
which you are interpreting as a loss, has actually
become gain. For only in this suffering am I now
able to reveal Myself to you in a way that you
have not previously known. You have called Me
Lord, but henceforth you shall know Me as the
Resurrection and the Life."

*Then they took away the stone from the
place where the dead was laid. And Jesus*

lifted up his eyes, and said, Father, I
thank thee that thou hast heard me. And
I knew that thou hearest me always:
but because of the people which stand
by I said it, that they may believe that
thou hast sent me. And when he thus
had spoken, he cried with a loud voice,
Lazarus, come forth. And he that was
dead came forth, bound hand and foot
with graveclothes: and his face was
bound about with a napkin. Jesus saith
unto them, Loose him, and let him go.
Then many of the Jews which came to
Mary, and had seen the things which
Jesus did, believed on him.
—John 11:41–45

Our time of mourning puts us in touch
with the eternal resources of God. We are made
open to God in ways we could never experience
apart from that mourning. We may not have
chosen this sorrow for our life, but as a result, we
are closer to God, and stronger because of the
strength He supplies. God provides this strength
to us in various ways. There is strength in the

assurance of forgiveness. There is strength in the peace of restored spiritual fellowship with the Lord. There is strength in the presence of the Holy Spirit Who comes alongside us in grief and glory to keep and to preserve us in the way of Christ-likeness. There is strength in the comfort of our spiritual family, who minister to us physically, emotionally, mentally, and spiritually; to encourage us and to heal. There is strength in the promises of God's Word, which assure us of His abiding presence within our hearts.

> *There is a connection between the strange providential circumstances allowed by God and what we know of Him, and we have to learn to interpret the mysteries of life in the light of our knowledge of God. Until we can come face to face with the deepest, darkest fact of life without damaging our view of God's character, we do not yet know Him.*—Oswald Chambers, *My Utmost for His Highest*

God will often wound before He heals. God will often abase before He exalts. Blessed are they that mourn.

As Christians, each of us possess the limitless treasure of God's grace, and that grace is both abounding and abiding in us. It's easy to be joyful when everything is great, but it's anything but joyful when your spouse is lying in a hospital bed, your child is sick, your family is separated, or your circumstance appears insurmountable. In such conditions, amazing grace can seem like a "maze of grace." At such times, we must follow the Lord Who is our WAY. We must cling to the One Who is TRUTH. We must believe in the One Who is not just an example of how to live, but LIFE itself. We must trust in the touch of an Almighty God Whose comfort encourages, Whose character strengthens. In Him, we discover the blessing of mourning. **In our reality, He is real.**

Epilogue

For I know the thoughts that I think toward you, saith the LORD, thoughts of peace, and not of evil, to give you an expected end. Then shall ye call upon me, and ye shall go and pray unto me, and I will hearken unto you. And ye shall seek me, and find me, when ye shall search for me with all your heart. And I will be found of you, saith the LORD: and I will turn away your captivity, and I will gather you from all the nations, and from all the places whither I have driven you,

> *saith the LORD; and I will bring you*
> *again into the place whence I caused you*
> *to be carried away captive.*
> —Jeremiah 29:11–14

The simplicity of appropriating God's grace may confound you. Maybe no one has ever shared with you the good news about Jesus Christ from the Bible. Maybe you have heard, but have never responded and have therefore rejected the grace of God. Jesus Christ came into this world to seek and to save the lost.

> *And Jesus answering said unto them,*
> *They that are whole need not a*
> *physician; but they that are sick. I came*
> *not to call the righteous, but sinners to*
> *repentance."*—Luke 5:31–32

This book has probably been put into your hands because you are suffering from sickness, loss, or adversity. Take this opportunity to let the words of the Great Physician, the One Who is able to make you spiritually whole, minister to you.

The Bible clearly expresses that, *"For all have sinned, and come short of the glory of God"* (Romans 3:23).

This only confirms a truth that our own life experiences verify as each of us can recall his own shortcomings. The Bible refers to these wrong choices and shortcomings as sin, and they are merely symptoms or indicators of a condition known as the sin nature. The consequence or natural outcome of this sin nature, if left untreated, is death. Not merely physical death, but spiritual death—separation from God.

> *But God commendeth* [He demonstrated] *his love toward us, in that, while we were yet sinners, Christ died for us.*—Romans 5:8

God's prescription for spiritual healing and wholeness is found only in His Son, Jesus Christ, who testified, *"Jesus saith unto him, I am the way, the truth, and the life: no man cometh unto the Father, but by me"* (John 14:6).

If you will confess with your mouth and believe with your heart the testimony of Scripture concerning the Lord Jesus Christ, then you shall be saved. What must you believe? You must believe that, *"For God so loved the world, that he gave his only begotten Son, that whosoever believeth in him should not perish, but have everlasting life"* (John 3:16).

You must accept, *"For I delivered unto you first of all that which I also received, how that Christ died for our sins according to the scriptures; And that he was buried, and that he rose again the third day according to the scriptures"* (1 Corinthians 15:3–4).

The substance of the Gospel is this: Christ took your place. He is your Substitute. He served the penalty for your sin and for the sin of the world on Calvary, and He asks you this one thing: believe in Me. We believe in Christ and confess that "[Jesus is] *the Christ, the Son of the living God"* (Matthew 16:16).

Our belief is the basis upon which we receive the free gift of God's grace, the promise of everlasting life, and the abiding presence of the Spirit of God, Who comes alongside us to comfort and instruct us in righteousness.

The Bible indicates that, *"No man can come to me* [Jesus], *except the Father which hath sent me*

draw him: and I will raise him up at the last day"
(John 6:44).

Right now you may be experiencing that drawing: that inclination, that desire to believe and be set free from the questions, doubts, and fear of death that enslave the soul. Your present condition is sin; the prognosis is salvation if you will believe in the Lord Jesus Christ. You may communicate your decision to accept Christ as your Saviour by talking to God through prayer.

> *Then shall ye call upon me, and ye shall go and pray unto me, and I will hearken unto you. And ye shall seek me, and find me, when ye shall search for me with all your heart.*—Jeremiah 29:12–13

And that's a promise and prescription on which you can depend.

> *Amazing Grace! How sweet the sound!*
> *That saved a wretch like me!*

John Newton wrote the words to this timeless song. In early life, he set sail on the high seas as a slave trader, and set a course for debauchery and degradation of himself and others. John Newton was an unlikely candidate for the pastorate, but an ideal candidate for God's grace. After his conversion, Newton became a powerful Gospel preacher and pastor, and served in that capacity for most of his life. At the age of eighty-two, Newton said, "My memory is nearly gone, but I remember two things: that I am a sinner, and that Christ is a great Saviour." No wonder he understood grace so well—the completely undeserved mercy and favor of God. We are told that the epitaph on Newton's tombstone reads as follows: "John Newton, Clerk, once an infidel and libertine, a servant of slaves in Africa, was, by the rich mercy of our Lord and Saviour Jesus Christ, preserved, restored, pardoned, and appointed to preach the faith he had long labored to destroy." But a far greater testimony outlives Newton in the greatest of the hundreds of hymns he wrote—**Amazing Grace**.

> *Amazing Grace! How sweet the sound!*
> *That saved a wretch like me!*
> *I once was lost, But now am found*
> *Was blind but now I see.*

In evil long I took delight
Unawed by shame or fear;
'Til a new object met my sight,
And stopped my wild career.

I saw One hanging on a tree,
In agonies and blood;
Who fixed His languid eyes on me
As near His cross I stood.

Sure, never 'til my latest breath,
Can I forget that look
It seemed to charge me with His death
Though not a word He spoke.

My conscience owned and felt the guilt,
And plunged me in despair;
I saw my sins His blood had shed,
And helped to nail Him there.

Alas, I knew not what I did,
But all my tears were vain;
Where could my trembling soul be hid,
For I the Lord had slain!

'Twas grace that taught my heart to fear,
And grace my fears relieved;

How precious did that grace appear
The hour I first believed!

Through many dangers, toils and snares
I have already come.
'Tis grace hath brought me safe thus far,
And grace will lead me home!

The Lord has promised good to me,
His Word my hope secures;
He will my shield and portion be,
As long as life endures!

Yes, when this flesh and heart shall fail,
And mortal life shall cease;
I shall possess within the veil,
A life of joy and peace!

The earth shall soon dissolve like snow,
The sun forbear to shine;
But God who called me here below
Shall be forever mine!

When we've been there ten thousand years,
Bright shining as the sun;
We've no less days to sing God's praise
Than when we first begun!

Other mini books available from Striving Together

These powerful little books make perfect gifts of encouragement!

What Is a Biblical Fundamentalist?
by Dr. Paul Chappell

Biblical fundamentalism is being redefined today. So, what exactly is a biblical fundamentalist? In these pages you will discover the history, the true definition, and the clear-cut beliefs of someone who believes the basic, central teachings of the Bible.

Discerning Alcohol
by Dr. Paul Chappell

Explore the Bible passages that speak about alcohol, gain insight to God's definition of alcohol, and understand what God says about this controversial subject. If you are struggling with understanding what God teaches on this subject, these pages will clearly and concisely cut to the very heart of the matter.

Your Pastor & You
by Dr. Paul Chappell and Cary Schmidt

God has given you a gift! A pastor—a loving under-shepherd to encourage, edify, and equip your life for spiritual growth and fruitfulness. In these pages, you will understand the blessings in store and the challenges ahead in your relationship with your pastor!

www.strivingtogether.com

For more information about our ministry visit:

www.strivingtogether.com
for helpful Christian resources

www.dailyintheword.org
for an encouraging word each day

www.lancasterbaptist.org
for information about Lancaster Baptist Church

www.wcbc.edu
for information about West Coast Baptist College